A Picnic for Two

2 two ● ●

I can see two apples.

2   apples

One apple is for you.

One apple is for me.

I can see two sandwiches.

2 sandwiches

One sandwich is for you.

One sandwich is for me.

I can see two little cakes.

2 cakes

One little cake is for you.

One little cake is for me.

We can see two apples,

and two sandwiches,

and two little cakes.

two   apples

two   sandwiches

two   cakes